W9-CXM-985

INSIDE THE WORLD OF SPORTS

LACROSSE

INSIDE THE WORLD OF SPORTS

AUTO RACING
BASEBALL
BASKETBALL
EXTREME SPORTS
FOOTBALL
GOLF
GYMNASTICS
ICE HOCKEY
LACROSSE
SOCCER
TENNIS
TRACK & FIELD
WRESTLING

INSIDE THE WORLD OF SPORTS

LACROSSE

by Andrew Luke

MASON CREST

Mason Crest
450 Parkway Drive, Suite D
Broomall, Pennsylvania 19008
(866) MCP-BOOK (toll free)

First printing
9 8 7 6 5 4 3 2 1

ISBN (hardback) 978-1-4222-3464-8
ISBN (series) 978-1-4222-3455-6
ISBN (ebook) 978-1-4222-8426-1

Cataloging-in-Publication Data on file with the Library of Congress

QR CODES AND LINKS TO THIRD-PARTY CONTENT

You may gain access to certain third-party content ("Third-Party Sites") by scanning and using the QR Codes that appear in this publication (the "QR Codes"). We do not operate or control in any respect any information, products, or services on such Third-Party Sites linked to by us via the QR Codes included in this publication and we assume no responsibility for any materials you may access using the QR Codes. Your use of the QR Codes may be subject to terms, limitations, or restrictions set forth in the applicable terms of use or otherwise established by the owners of the Third-Party Sites. Our linking to such Third-Party Sites via the QR Codes does not imply an endorsement or sponsorship of such Third-Party Sites, or the information, products or services offered on or through the Third-Party Sites, nor does it imply an endorsement or sponsorship of this publication by the owners of such Third-Party Sites.

CONTENTS

KEY ICONS TO LOOK FOR:

Words to understand: These words with their easy-to-understand definitions will increase the reader's understanding of the text while building vocabulary skills.

Educational Videos: Readers can view videos by scanning our QR codes, providing them with additional educational content to supplement the text. Examples include news coverage, moments in history, speeches, iconic sports moments and much more!

Text-dependent questions: These questions send the reader back to the text for more careful attention to the evidence presented there.

Research projects: Readers are pointed toward areas of further inquiry connected to each chapter. Suggestions are provided for projects that encourage deeper research and analysis.

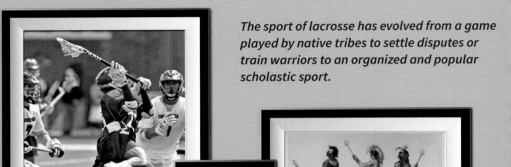

The sport of lacrosse has evolved from a game played by native tribes to settle disputes or train warriors to an organized and popular scholastic sport.

CHAPTER 1

LACROSSE'S GREATEST MOMENTS

North Americans have been playing the game of lacrosse for unknown centuries. The game is a time-honored pursuit of the native people of the continent. The first European explorers of the lands that now make up Canada and the United States found that the native tribes would play for days at a time, using their crude sticks to chase the ball over great distances in their bare feet.

Lacrosse has come a long way since settlers adopted and refined the native game into a modern sport that is much beloved and ardently followed at the high school and college levels in both countries. In the United States (according to U.S. Lacrosse, the sport's U.S. governing body), the number of people playing lacrosse has risen steadily, from about 250,000 in 2001 to more than 650,000 in 2011, a 160 percent increase. Projections show that the number of total players could eclipse one million in 2016. From 2010 to 2011 alone, participation in youth lacrosse (players under age 15) was up 11.3 percent.

On the college front, the National Collegiate Athletic Association also reports increased participation. There are more than 60 NCAA Division I men's programs, and hundreds of others in Divisions II and III. Administrators point to the growing popularity at the youth level as a reason why they added varsity lacrosse at their school. With the addition of lacrosse in the Big Ten Conference in 2014, the sport is now sponsored in two of the Power Five conferences, along with longtime lacrosse powerhouse the Atlantic Coast Conference.

The Big Ten, with its own national cable outlet, gives the sport unprecedented exposure. By luring 12-time NCAA finalist Maryland away from the ACC and adding Johns Hopkins University, the crown jewel of lacrosse schools, as an affiliate, the Big Ten gave itself instant credibility in the sport, and opened up hundreds more scholarships for the sport, ensuring lacrosse's viability at lower levels.

As the college game continues to grow and thrive, so will the number of great moments it produces for fans that marvel at the skill of these players and the drama it can produce.

Air Gait Goal

In 1988, Syracuse played Pennsylvania in an NCAA men's Division I semifinal. The Orangemen were led by superstar sophomore attackman Gary Gait, and in this game, he showed why he was one of the best in the sport.

Trailing 2-1 in the second quarter, Gait had possession of the ball behind the Penn net. The goalie watched him over his shoulder, waiting for Gait to pass the ball out front or to try and come around the side of the net. Instead, Gait ran straight at the back of the net, planted his left foot just outside the crease line and leapt in the air toward the net. He reached over the crossbar and stuffed the ball in behind the stunned goalie, who had never seen anything like the "Air Gait." Gait scored another of his record nine goals by using the move a second time in that game, which Syracuse won 11-10. The move was eventually outlawed in NCAA competition.

Hidden Ball Trick

Gait was also adept at another move that is still legal, and he demonstrated it the following year in a match against the Naval Academy. He had the help of his twin brother Paul, who also played for Syracuse. The Orangemen played Navy in the quarterfinal round of the 1989 NCAA Division 1 playoffs.

On a dead ball play, Syracuse had possession following a Navy goal and the twins met at midfield to initiate the start of play. With their backs turned to the Navy defense, Paul appeared to transfer the ball from his stick to Gary's. Instead, he did a quick swirl of his stick, and the ball remained in his webbing. The two then turned to start the play, with Gary running left at the defense, pretending to cradle a ball in his stick. Meanwhile, Paul casually walked to the right, holding his stick like he would if it were empty. The ploy worked perfectly. As Navy watched Gary, Paul suddenly fired the ball from 30 yards out right into the goal. The Navy goalie never saw the ball go in. Syracuse won 18-11, advancing to its second straight championship.

1989 NCAA National Championship

In that 1989 championship game, the Gaits and top-ranked Syracuse faced second seed Johns Hopkins. The Orangemen had lost just a single match in the last two seasons coming into this championship contest. That was a loss to Johns Hopkins to start the 1989 season.

The championship game was close throughout between the two evenly matched teams. After the third quarter, JHU led 11-9, and it looked like the Blue Jays might win their fifth title of the decade. In the fourth quarter, however, Syracuse showed why they were the defending champions. Rodney Dumpson quickly scored to make it 11-10. A few minutes later, Gary Gait scooped up a loose ball in the Blue Jays' end and rushed at the net. Checked from behind, he shot while falling and managed to score the tying goal with just over 12 minutes left. Syracuse kept coming, with John Zulberti scoring the go-ahead goal on a beautiful diving play from the edge of the crease. When Dumpson scored his second goal of the quarter and the fourth unanswered tally to make it 13-11, Syracuse seemed fated to win. Hopkins rallied furiously, but Syracuse held on to win 13-12 in what many experts consider to be the greatest lacrosse game ever played.

Moe Is Money

Legendary coach of the Princeton Tigers, Bill Tierney, took over the men's lacrosse program in 1988. The Tigers had never won a NCAA Championship, with the program's last year of glory coming with an Intercollegiate Lacrosse Association Championship in 1953. Tierney turned the program around, leading his team to five national championships in the 1990s. The run began in the 1992 NCAA D1 playoffs.

Third-ranked Princeton got to the final against top-ranked Syracuse, which was playing its fourth final in five seasons. The underdog Tigers fought hard to get the game to overtime at 9-9. No one could score in the first overtime. Princeton gained possession off the faceoff to open the second overtime period when the ball squirted away from the battling centers to attackman Andy Moe. Moe had already scored three of Princeton's nine goals and looked dangerous as he scooped up the ball and sprinted down the right side with two defenders giving chase. They never caught him, and nine seconds into the period he fired the ball past the Syracuse keeper for his fourth goal and the win. Tierney would win a sixth championship for Princeton in 2001, and the seventh of his career with Denver University in 2015.

The Tenth Title

Johns Hopkins' lacrosse program has more national championships than any other but most of these came in the pre-NCAA era when JHU won 35 titles. They also have nine NCAA Championships, however, which was tied for the modern era record with Syracuse until 2009. Syracuse had success under coach Roy Simmons Jr. and the Gait brothers (five titles from 1988-1995), but they were equally dominant in the 2000s when led by coach John Desko. Desko took over from Simmons in 1999 and coached the Orange to four NCAA Championships in nine seasons going into the 2009 championship game.

Second-ranked Syracuse trailed the fifth-seeded Big Red 9-6 with less than four minutes to play in the final, and it looked like an upset was brewing. The Orange showed their mettle, however, scoring two quick goals 51 seconds apart to make it a one-goal game. It was still 9-8, however, with the clock running down under 15 seconds to play when a Cornell turnover at midfield gave Syracuse one last chance. The Orange scooped up the loose ball, and after a desperate, deflected pass found star attackman Kenny Nims at the edge of the Cornell crease, he buried it with just four seconds left to force overtime. Attackman Cody Jamieson scored 1:20 into overtime to give the Orange NCAA title number 10.

Duke Wins First NCAA Championship

The following season, Duke University was looking for NCAA Championship number one. Better known for basketball, the Blue Devil lacrosse program had come to prominence in 2006 when three of its players were falsely accused of rape, and the school canceled its season. This overshadowed the work done by Duke coach Mike Pressler, who took over the job in 1991 and turned the program around. The Blue Devils made the NCAA tournament in 1992 and won its first tournament game in 1995, leading up to an appearance in the finals in 2005.

During the scandal in 2006, the school forced Pressler to resign. His job went to John Danowski, who led the team back to the final in 2007. As in 2005, Duke lost, but Danowski persevered, and in 2010 made the final again, with the help of some fifth-year seniors whose eligibility was extended after they lost their freshman season in the 2006 scandal. This time, in a tense 6-5 overtime game, Duke won its first title over Notre Dame, the ultimate justice for those seniors. Danowski then led the Blue Devils to back-to-back titles in 2013 and 2014, cementing a new association for Duke lacrosse: national champions.

"An Indian Ball Play" is a work by early 19th-century artist George Catlin depicting native tribes in a massive lacrosse match.

 Words to Understand:

avenge: to take vengeance on behalf of

endurance: the ability or strength to continue or last, especially despite fatigue, stress, or other adverse conditions; stamina

arbitrating: deciding between opposing or contending parties or sides

CHAPTER 2

WAR GAMES

There is no definitive moment or recorded event that tells us when the very first stick-and-ball game came to be, and who invented it, or why it came to be. What we do know is that references and depictions of such games go back for thousands of years.

THE ORIGIN OF LACROSSE

The game of lacrosse is thought to have evolved from games that, based on the study of ruins, appear to have been similar to those played by tribes in South America and Mexico.

The first actual accounts, however, of a game that closely resembles the modern sport of lacrosse are typically associated with the tribes of North America. There are various myths surrounding its origin. The Menomini legend tells the story of Manabozho, who arranged for an other worldly lacrosse match to be played so he could lure the underworld gods into the open to **avenge** his brother's death. The Ojibwa believe the idea for the game came to a boy in a dream.

LIP SERVICE

Word of mouth was the method used to maintain the continuity of the game of lacrosse as it developed, persisting in stories of great victories. In the 18th century, French Jesuit missionaries in Quebec, Canada, that interacted with the natives began to record the stories and observations of actual games, a function of their training to be mindful of every detail of the cultures they attempted to influence.

In the 1830s, Pennsylvania artist and author George Catlin headed west to chronicle the life of what he saw as the disappearing Native American people. Among the more than 600 works he created during and after his years on the plains were paintings of tribes playing the game that the Jesuits described a hundred years earlier. One of his most vivid paintings is titled *An Indian Ball Play*.

PREPARING TO FIGHT

The games Catlin witnessed were primarily staged as training events for young braves. They were training not to become star lacrosse players, but rather for battles against rival tribes. Often violent and lengthy in duration, the natives considered the game to be excellent for developing strength and **endurance**. Players were typically forbidden to eat during games that could last for three days, simulating, in theory, the conditions faced by warriors in combat. Prior to matches, the braves could only consume meat from fierce animals like the bear, not from timid animals like the rabbit.

For tribe leaders, lacrosse served as part of effective battle strategy. In June of 1763, unarmed Ojibwa warriors staged a game within sight of the walls of Fort Michilimackinac, in Michigan. As the game raged on, the soldiers at the fort, most of them unarmed, wandered out to get a better look at the spectacle of the natives battling each other, leaving the gate open. Slowly, the play moved closer and closer to the fort. Before the soldiers realized what was happening, players became warriors, rushing the soldiers and overcoming them before they could get back through the gate, and eventually capturing the fort.

George Catlin was a 19th-century painter and writer who wa the first white man to create images of the tribes of the Grea Plains, including several of the natives playing lacrosse.

SETTLE IT ON THE FIELD

Lacrosse was also used as a means of **arbitrating** disputes between tribes. In these contests designed to resolve conflicts, there were no rules. Players could tackle, trip or kick opponents or, more effectively, smash them with their sticks. Serious injuries were very common, as the natives wore minimal clothing and no protective gear at all.

The resolution of whatever was in dispute between tribes was often not the only thing at stake in these lacrosse battles. Wagering was common. Catlin, in one of his paintings, depicts a Choctaw woman whipping her husband to inspire him to fight to protect all the goods they had bet on the outcome of the game.

THE FIELD OF PLAY

Preparations for a match were thorough. As the players were all barefoot, the field selected for the match was first cleared of stones, raked clear with moose antlers. Players from the visiting tribe would use the field as their campground during the two or three days of competition. Often 1,000 players would take part, allowing for large-scale substitution of the 100 or so players that were on the field during play.

Fields were also selected for their proximity to streams or other water sources to keep the players hydrated. The boundaries of fields varied widely, with no sidelines, and the distance between goals ranged from 500 yards to several miles.

Lacrosse was played with a variety of balls, ranging from stuffed animal hide balls to ones made of solid wood or clay. Sticks also varied widely from tribe to tribe. Some had pockets enclosed completely by wood, while others used twisted bark or leather strips to form a net. Tribes in what is now the Northeastern U.S. and Eastern Ontario, Canada, preferred unenclosed pocket sticks with crude netting. This version of the stick eventually evolved into the modern stick used by today's high school and college players.

Lacrosse sticks have evolved from twisted bark netting on wooden frames to synthetic nets on titanium frames.

"Ball-play Dance" by George Catlin, 1834. Before the match, players and their supporters passed the night in singing, dancing, and soliciting divine support.

Text-Dependent Questions:

Who is the Pennsylvania artist and author that headed west to chronicle the life of what he saw as the disappearing Native American people and came across the game of lacrosse?

What was the main purpose for Native American tribes who used the practice of lacrosse?

Describe the earliest fields used for playing lacrosse by Native American tribes.

Research Project:

ompare the origin of lacrosse to that of other sports such as football, occer, or hockey. Are there any commonalities to how or why the orts began?

Sioux Playing Ball 1843

Words to Understand:

shaman: a person who acts as an intermediary between the natural and supernatural wo using magic to cure illness, foretell the future, control spiritual forces, and so on

cupped: hollowed out like a cup; cup shaped

exhibition matches: unofficial matches played under regular game conditions between professional teams

CHAPTER 3

MORE THAN A GAME

Among the native North American tribes, the game of lacrosse held much significance. From battle training method to arbitration vehicle, it played a significant part in the culture of native people.

CEREMONY FOR THE SPIRITS

Lacrosse was also important in the religious ceremonies of many tribes. Beliefs differed from tribe to tribe, but most held to a central belief that a magical and mysterious spirit power controlled the universe and their lives. This force had many names: manito, orenda, and wokonda.

Religious ceremonies were designed to gain the favor of these spirits, whether to bring success in hunting or to yield a bountiful crop. Many tribes incorporated lacrosse games as part of ceremonies marking seasonal change, like the Green Corn Ceremony of the Oklahoma Creek people.

Lacrosse was played as part of the funeral ceremonies for gifted players, who were often buried with their lacrosse stick. In some tribes, such as the Huron, games were also played as curing ceremonies to ask the spirits to provide healing for the sick.

THE SHAMAN ADVANTAGE

In an effort to gain the upper hand on the teams from other tribes, many employed the services of a **shaman**, or medicine man, religious practitioners tribes believed could communicate with spirits. Shaman were asked to do everything from creating dolls to represent the opposing tribe designed to bewitch them, to "doctoring balls", which meant adding materials with magical powers to their stuffing.

Other tactics included the blessing of the lacrosse sticks and rituals like the Cherokee's "going to the water." In this ritual, players would stand on a riverbank with sticks held in front of them while a shaman prayed over differently colored beads representing his tribe's success and the failure of the opponent. The players would then dip their sticks into the stream and kiss the wet instrument.

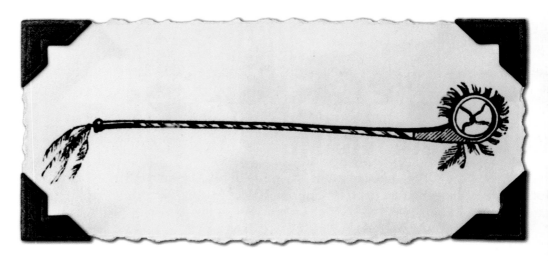

Tribes would often adorn their lacrosse sticks with items such as eagle feathers and other charms believed to bring physical advantages to the user.

NATIVE SKILL

Blessed, bewitched, or otherwise, the players of these native tribes developed high levels of skill in lacrosse. Sticks were often adorned with symbols like eagle feathers, which were believed to grant the user the sharp eyesight and fast, powerful motion of the bird. Whether assisted by these charms or by hours of play and practice, players became adept at the game in its various forms.

Some tribes, like the Iroquois, Cherokee, and Seminole, played a double-stick version of the game. In this variation, players carried a stick in each hand. These sticks were typically just over two feet long, shorter than those in the single-stick game. One stick was about six inches shorter than the other, with a smaller pocket for the ball. Players would carry the ball **cupped** between the pockets of the two sticks. Players were adept at running and maneuvering while carrying the ball in this fashion. In native games, the ball rarely touched the ground, and one rule was strictly observed universally by all tribes: it was forbidden to touch the ball with the hand.

EVOLUTION

Forbidding the touching of the ball was the only real rule the game of lacrosse had for centuries. As the French and English settlers of North America came into contact with and adapted the game from its native form, more formal rules evolved.

It was not until 1867, however, that the first formal rules for the game of lacrosse were adopted. On July 1, 1867, Canada was officially declared a nation and, in conjunction, officially declared lacrosse to be the new nation's official sport.

THE MODERN GAME

Dr. William Beers, a dentist from Montreal, compiled the first collection of formal regulations. In 1867, he founded the Canadian National Lacrosse Foundation, which used his rules as its basis. He grew up playing the game, and his rules reflected an emphasis on team play. Beers' major rules were these:

- A team could field 12 players, with no substitutions.

- The first team to lead by three goals or to reach five goals won.

- Goals were 6'x6', and recommended to be 200 feet apart.

- Balls could be no less than eight inches but no more than 10 inches in circumference.

- Two on-field officials, called umpires, were stationed one at each goal while a referee followed the play up and down the field.

- Only the goalkeeper could touch the ball with a hand. Otherwise it was a foul. Other fouls included holding, tripping, making verbal threats, hitting opponents with the stick, or throwing the stick.

THE GAME SPREADS

The popularity of lacrosse in Canada was exported by Native American troupes that traveled around playing **exhibition** matches. In 1867, one such troupe traveled to France, Ireland, Scotland, and England. Another troupe played an exhibition match at Saratoga Springs, New York, on August 7, 1867, which was covered by an American newspaper. This is the first known mention of the game in the American press.

On October 16, 1867, a native troupe played an exhibition at a baseball tournament in Troy, New York. Again, the local papers covered the match, and this time, it led to the founding of the first lacrosse club in the United States, called the Mohawk Club of Troy.

Dr. William Beers

Vancouver Lacrosse Club, Minto Cup holders, in a 1912 team photo

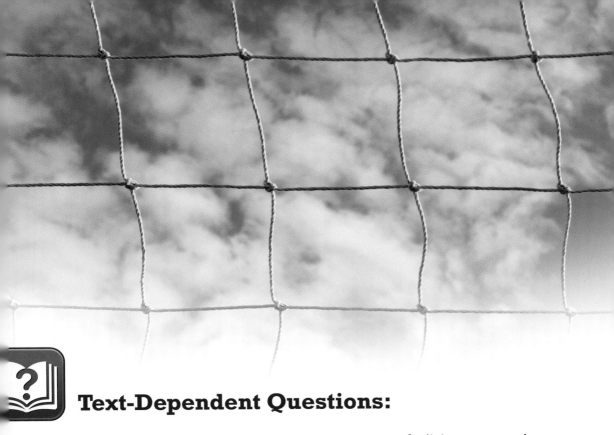

Text-Dependent Questions:

Cite some examples of how tribes used lacrosse games as part of religious ceremonies.

Who created the first formal collection of rules for the game of lacrosse?

What led to the founding of the first lacrosse club in the United States?

Research Project:

ake a closer look at the use of lacrosse in religious ceremonies, and compare this to the
ligious ceremonies you are familiar with today. How would it be seen to use a sport as part
a religious ceremony in the 21st century?

A 1955 college game between Maryland and Johns Hopkins

 Words to Understand:

phenomenon: something that is impressive or extraordinary

intercollegiate: taking place between or participating in activities between different colle

hiatus: a break or interruption in the continuity of work, a series, action, and so on

bodychecking: obstructing another player

CHAPTER 4

THE COLLEGE SPORT

In the late 1860s, lacrosse clubs sprang up across the Northeast and Midwest. By 1876, the game was such a **phenomenon** that Beers was invited to organize an exhibition match to be played before Queen Victoria at Windsor Castle in England. That same year, 8,000 spectators turned up for an exhibition match in Newport, Rhode Island. Following the match, the *New York Herald* declared lacrosse to be "the most remarkable, versatile, and exciting of all games of ball." The following year, lacrosse would transform into a sport.

INTERCOLLEGIATE LACROSSE

In the autumn of 1877, at the beginning of another school year at college campuses in the Northeastern U.S., a lacrosse match was played between teams representing Manhattan College and New York University. NYU won 2-0 in a match that was called due to darkness.

This match was a momentous occasion in lacrosse because U.S. college players would go on to transform the game forever. The sport spread into Maryland and New Jersey, and in 1882, the Intercollegiate Lacrosse Association was formed. Yale, Harvard, and Princeton were among the schools that dominated early **intercollegiate** lacrosse play.

BUMPS IN THE ROAD

Despite coming to prominence at about the same time as the other major sports, lacrosse had a harder time growing. Experts speculate that the difficulty in mastering the stick skills required for lacrosse made the sport less popular than baseball and football.

At Yale, Harvard and Princeton, administrators became reluctant to divert star athletes from football, baseball, crew and track and field, and all three schools eventually dropped lacrosse. By the turn of the century, however, the game found its footing at smaller colleges throughout the region, and the sport also grew in the Midwest and the South.

JOHNS HOPKINS BLACK AND BLUE

Lacrosse also took root in the Baltimore area, especially at Johns Hopkins University, where the school's lacrosse team (the Black and Blue, named for their uniform colors) had persevered since 1883. Unlike at its three Ivy League competitors, the sport thrived at JHU, and many of lacrosse's innovations originated there.

A player from the lacrosse powerhouse Johns Hopkins University Blue Jays in action. JHU has won the most national collegiate titles.

In 1898, freshman Robert Abercrombie was a center on the school's second national championship team (JHU has won 44 national collegiate titles through 2015) and was captain of two more championship squads in 1899 and 1900. Abercrombie would go on to serve as president of the ILA, but is best known for innovating the use of a shorter stick for attackmen, making short passes more effective. He is also credited with being the first to put a net on the goalposts.

LACROSSE AND THE OLYMPICS

Lacrosse was selected as an exhibition (non-medal) sport at both the 1904 and 1908 Olympic Games. After a 20-year **hiatus**, the sport was afforded the same status again at the Olympics in 1928 and 1932. In both years, the lacrosse team from Johns Hopkins (now called the Blue Jays) was chosen to serve as the U.S. Olympic lacrosse team, and in 1932, Johns Hopkins standout attackman Jack Turnbull and goalie Fritz Stude were

e U.S. team's best players, leading the
ue Jays to an undefeated season. Their
precedented success was illuminated
 the spotlight of the Olympic Games and
rust lacrosse into the national spotlight.

omen took up the sport around the
rn of the century. The first organized
omen's clubs appeared in Baltimore
1926, then in Philadelphia and
w York. The U.S. Women's Lacrosse
sociation was formed in 1931, and the
st championship game for women was
ayed in 1933.

EW RULES
e year 1933 also saw the sport
nsform due to its first significant rule

*Women have been playing
organized lacrosse since 1926.*

anges to the men's game. The number of players on the field for each team was reduced
om 12 to 10 (women still play with a dozen). The distance between goals, which had increased
om Beers' recommended 200 feet to 330 feet, was reduced again to 240 feet, with 20 yards
om the back of each goal to the end boundary. The 10 positions that remained were three
tackmen, three midfielders (middies), three defenders and a goalkeeper.

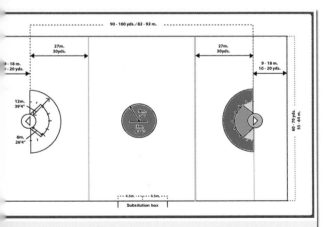

*Women's lacrosse field dimensions based on 2007
IFWLA women's lacrosse rules*

THE MODERN GAME
The three attackmen are comprised
of two wingers and a center. Similar
to hockey, which borrowed the
tradition from lacrosse, the game
begins with a battle for the ball in the
middle of the field between the two
centers called a face-off.

The origin of the face-off to begin
lacrosse games is untraceable,
but there are written accounts of
games from the late 18th century
that describe face-offs as the ritual
used to begin games between Native
American tribes.

Players carry or pass the ball with netted sticks and attempt to throw or kick the ball into the opposing goal. Lacrosse is a full-contact sport, and **bodychecking** is allowed, but not every kind of contact is legal, and like soccer, fouls can be called. Like football, games are played in four 15-minute quarters (women play two 30-minute halves).

MODERN EQUIPMENT

In the 1960s, wooden sticks gave way to synthetic varieties and now are made of lightweight aluminum or titanium. Attackmen use the longest sticks (up to 72") while defenders' sticks can be as short as 40".

Protective gear is mandatory. Male players are required to wear a helmet complete with full facemask, a mouthpiece, and padded gloves.

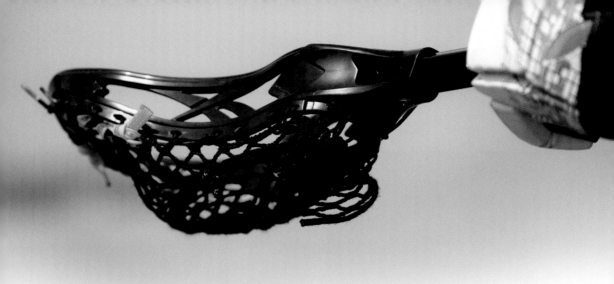

Text-Dependent Questions:

In 1876 which newspaper declared lacrosse to be "the most remarkable, versatile, and exciting of all games of ball"?

When was the U.S. Women's Lacrosse Association formed?

When did wooden sticks give way to synthetic varieties such as aluminum and titanium?

Research Project:

ook back at lacrosse equipment from the beginning of the sport to today. Create a collage images to show how the equipment has changed over the years. Research why these anges were made, and provide evidence to show the effect these equipment changes ve had on the game.

Gary Gait during the 2006 World Lacrosse Championship gold medal game

Words to Understand:

innovators: those who introduce something new or make changes in anything establishe[d]

dominance: rule, control, authority

inaugural: the first in a series of similar events

CHAPTER 5

THE FAMILY GAME

When the rules of the sport changed in 1933, Jack Turnbull and his Johns Hopkins University Blue Jays had just represented the U.S. at the 1932 Olympics in Los Angeles. Turnbull was called 'the Babe Ruth of lacrosse," a reference to the superstar baseball slugger for the New York Yankees at the time.

THE TURNBULLS

Turnbull inherited his athletic gifts from his father Doug, who starred at football, baseball, cricket, tennis, and golf. Jack's older brother, Doug Jr., was also a star athlete who took up lacrosse at age 10. He blazed the trail Jack would follow, starring in lacrosse through high school and at Johns Hopkins.

Doug was a great player, but Jack was a superstar for the Blue Jays, which he led to two consecutive undefeated seasons, in 1931 and 1932, the year he served as captain.

After playing together at the Olympics, the brothers joined a Baltimore-based club team called the Mt. Washington Wolfpack, where they played for 10 years, up until America's involvement in World War II began. Jack enlisted in the Air Force and became a bomber pilot. He was killed over Germany in October of 1944. Today, the Jack Turnbull Award is presented to the top attackman in each NCAA division.

THE GAIT TWINS

Another set of dominant lacrosse brothers was Gary and Paul Gait. These siblings are twins from Victoria, British Columbia, who came to the U.S. in 1988 to play for legendary coach Roy Simmons Jr. at Syracuse University. The brothers were **innovators** in the sport, playing a wide-open, offensive style. In their four-year college career, they won three championships and were the cornerstones of the undefeated 1990 team, which many experts call the best team of all time. The 1990 season ended in the third straight championship for Simmons and the Gaits, but was later turned to disappointment as the title was vacated when the NCAA discovered that Simmons' wife had co-signed a car loan for Paul.

The Gaits are credited with increasing the exposure of lacrosse to a broader audience with their high-scoring **dominance**. They set several collegiate scoring records, were multiple-time All-Americans and went on to have successful professional careers. Lacrosse participation in the U.S. doubled during the 1980s.

THE COACHES

Simmons Jr. was the reason the highly sought after Gaits chose to play at Syracuse. He learned everything he knew about the sport from his father, Roy Simmons Sr. Simmons was a football player at Syracuse when he first encountered lacrosse there in 1922. He saw non-scholarship players with funny sticks running around with the football players' castoff jerseys. Simmons was intrigued but concentrated on football, in which he captained the Orangemen to an 8-1-1 record. But he also kept an eye on the lacrosse team, and when he noticed that they went 17-0 on their season, he signed up.

Simmons excelled at the sport, becoming a two-time lacrosse All-American and winning two national championships. When he graduated, he did not leave campus, instead staying on as the boxing, lacrosse, and assistant football coach. It was in lacrosse where his influence was most felt, and not only because he won a championship in 1957. Simmons believed in and practiced equality among all people, and treated minority athletes the same as any other athlete. Only the best players made the team, and Simmons did not care what those players looked like, a rarity in those times. He was instrumental in getting NFL Hall of Famer Jim Brown admitted to Syracuse, using lacrosse recruiting money to give him a scholarship the football program refused to. Brown was an All-American in both football and lacrosse while at Syracuse from 1953-1956. Simmons Jr. took over as lacrosse coach when his father retired in 1970, and won six championships.

BOB SCOTT

One of Simmons Sr.'s main rivals was Johns Hopkins coach Bob Scott, who coached the Blue Jays for 20 seasons from 1955-1974, winning six ILA Championships and an NCAA Championship as well.

THE PLAYERS DECIDE

Scott's teams won the last four ILA titles before the NCAA assumed control of the collegiate lacrosse championship. Under the ILA system, winners were decided by a vote, much like the NCAA did with football until 2014. For lacrosse, when the NCAA took over in 1971, they instituted a championship playoff tournament. Coach Richie Moran of Cornell celebrated this decision, as his team was not one of three ILA determined co-champions in 1970, despite an undefeated season.

Moran's Big Red squad demonstrated how good they were by winning the **inaugural** championship tournament in 1971. In the mid-1970s, they were even better, winning a record 42 straight games and two national titles in 1976 and 1977.

PROFESSIONAL LACROSSE

While lacrosse thrives as a high school and college game, it has had limited success as a professional sport. Major League Lacrosse is a professional league that started in 2001. In 2016, it had nine teams and has had as many as ten but as few as six.

The National Lacrosse League is a pro league for box lacrosse, a shrunken variation of the sport played in hockey arenas with teams of six. The league had nine teams in 2016 but has had as many as 13.

Many of today's top college lacrosse stars go on to play in both leagues, but the NCAA level is where they make their name in the sport.

The Rochester Rattlers (gold) vs. the Long Island Lizards (white) at PAETEC Park in 2008

Text-Dependent Questions:

Who was called "the Babe Ruth of lacrosse"?

Name the two brothers who came to the United States in 1988 from Canada to play for Coach Roy Simmons Jr. at Syracuse University.

When did Major League Lacrosse begin as a professional league?

Research Project:

Take a closer look at Major League Lacrosse, and compare it to the most popular and successful major league sports across the globe. What do you think needs to be done to grow the league? Share your suggestions on how to increase popularity of the professional sport.

Matt Danowski

Words to Understand:

prolific: producing a large amount of something

prowess: great ability or skill

accolades: awards or expressions of praise

CHAPTER 6

MODERN-DAY STARS

Whether it is at the NCAA or MLL level, the superstars of modern lacrosse have ever increasing opportunities to display their skills. From the edge of the opponent's crease to defending their own, today's top players compete at the highest athletic level.

FORWARDS

Hailing from the Onondaga Nation, NY, Lyle Thompson entered the University of Albany in 2012, where he played midfield as a freshman and scored just 38 points. Thompson moved to attack for his remaining seasons and posted point totals of 113, 128 and 121. His 128 points is the record for NCAA single-season points. His career totals are 175 goals and a record 225 assists for 400 points (also a record). Thompson was both NCAA attacker and player of the year in 2014 and 2015.

Cornell's Rob Pannell also won two Lt. Raymond Enners Awards for NCAA Most Outstanding Player (2011 and 2013). He won the Jack Turnbull Award for attacker of the year twice as well (2010 and 2011). His 354 points are second in history only to Thompson. Pannell was the first pick in the MLL draft and was league Rookie of the Year in 2013. He led the NY Lizards to the title in 2015.

Lyle Thompson

Duke University's Matt Danowski is also in the 150/150 club, with a career scoring line of 170-183-353, third best in history to Pannell by a single point. A four-time All-American from

2004-2008, Danowski terrorized defenses, winning Turnbull awards 2005 and 2007. In 2007, he also wor the Enners Award as the nation's to player, a feat he repeated in 2008. Danowski went on to MLL, where h became a six-time All-Star.

Danowski's teammate, Canadian-born Zack Greer, is the most **prolifi** goal scorer in men's NCAA lacrosse history. His 206 goals are the most ever, as he is the only player to hav scored more than 200. In 2007, Gre scored 67 goals to win the Turnbul even though Danowski won the Enners at the forward position. As a pro, Greer took his goal-scoring **prowess** indoors to the NLL box lacrosse league, starring for the Edmonton Rush.

Jordan Wolf

Jordan Wolf is only third on the all-time scoring list at Duke behind Danowski and Greer, but that puts the Wynnewood, PA, native at 11th in career points with 303. He is 7th in career goals with 185. Wolf was a big part of winning back-to-back national championships at Duke in 2013 and 2014, scoring six points and the game-winning goal to claim the championship game MVP award in 2014. In his second pro season, Wolf was named MLL Offensive Player of the Year.

41

MIDFIELDERS

Paul Rabil had a standout NCAA career at Johns Hopkins from 2005-2008. As a freshman, he was part of the 2005 NCAA Championship team. His Blue Jays won another title in 2007. In 2007, he won the Lt. Donald McLaughlin Jr. Award as the NCAA Most Outstanding Midfielder. As a pro, he has won three MLL Offensive Player of the Year awards in 2009, 2011 and 2012. Rabil is a two-time league champion, two-time MLL MVP, and the single season points record holder.

Rabil's JHU teammate Kyle Harrison is no stranger to winning awards and championships. A key part of that 2005 Blue Jays national championship run, Harrison won the McLaughlin Award that season, his second consecutive McLaughlin win. Harrison also won the Enners Award in 2005, as well as the Tewaaraton Trophy, a Player of the Year award typically given to the MOP of the post season. As a pro, he was the number one pick in the MLL draft in 2005 and is a four-time MLL All-Star.

Seattle native Peter Baum won both the Enners and the Tewaaraton as a junior at Colgate in 2012. He scored 96 points that season, playing all but three games at forward, out of his natural midfield position. When he played in the midfield, he was steady as a rock, putting up two 34-goal, 49-point seasons as a sophomore and a senior. Baum was selected as the number one pick in the 2013 MLL draft. He was a 2015 MLL All-Star.

Max Seibald of Cornell was the McLaughlin, Enners and Tewaaraton winner as a senior in 2009, capping a brilliant NCAA career. That season he led the Big Red to the NCAA Championship game, but Cornell lost to Syracuse in overtime, the only loss of the season for the Big Red. Seibald was selected in the first round of the 2009 MLL draft. He scored a career-high 39 points in 2012 and was a 2015 MLL All-Star.

Seibald's fellow 2015 MLL All-Star, East Meadow, NY, native Tom Schreiber, played his NCAA lacrosse at Princeton from 2011 to 2014. Schreiber was the Ivy League Rookie of the Year in 2011, then a First Team All-American his last three years. He won back-to-back McLaughlin Awards in 2013 and 2014 and ended his career at Princeton as the only midfielder in Ivy League history with at least 100 goals and 90 assists. Schreiber was taken first overall in the 2014 MLL draft.

Kyle Harrison

Peter Baum

DEFENSE

Tucker Durkin was a starter from the moment he arrived on campus at Johns Hopkins after being a two-time All-American at LaSalle College High near Philadelphia. Playing for coach Dave Pietramala, a former Hopkins defender, and Enners Award winner, Durkin thrived. He was named First Team All-American in his junior and senior years when he also won the William C. Schmeisser Award as the NCAA's best defenseman. As a pro, Durkin was named an MLL All-Star in each of his first two seasons.

When Durkin arrived at JHU in 2010, he filled the void in the defense that was created when Michael Evans left the year before. Evans had been that dependable presence on the Hopkins back line from 2006-2009, helping the Blue Jays reach back-to-back national championship games in 2007 and 2008. JHU won the championship over Duke in 2007. In 2009, he won the Schmeisser Award. As a pro, Evans is a six-time MLL All-Star and has won three league championships.

When Evans left the NCAA for MLL, the mantle of top NCAA defender went to North Carolina's Ryan Flanagan. Flanagan came to UNC in 2008 from West Islip, NY, as a highly recruited defender with size (6'6", 220 lbs.). As a junior, he was named First Team All-American and became a Schmeisser Award winner. After serving as co-captain of the Tar Heels in his senior year, Flanagan turned pro and is a four-time MLL All-Star.

Joe Fletcher of the MLL's NY Lizards is an MLL All-Star with a bright future. Not only was he named to the 2015 All-Star team in just his second season, but he was also named MLL Defensive Player of the Year. Fletcher's professional success comes on the heels of a standout college career at Loyola. As a junior with the Greyhounds in 2013, Fletcher was named First Team All-American. As a senior, he won the Schmeisser as top NCAA defender, foreshadowing his garnering the same **accolades** as a pro.

Like Fletcher, Michael Manley is a 2015 MLL All-Star, who also won MLL Defensive Player of the Year. Manley earned the award in 2014 with Rochester. The year 2014 was first of back-to-back appearances for Manley and Rochester in the MLL Championship game, but the Rattlers came up short both times. Losing championships was foreign to Manley in college, where he helped Duke to their first-ever championship in 2010. Manley was the first-round pick of the Rattlers in 2012.

GOAL
Drew Adams did not have the most accomplished NCAA career at Penn State. He played for the Nittany Lions from 2006-2009. He was never a First Team All-American and was never a candidate for an Ensign C. Markland Kelly Jr. Award for top NCAA goalie. He had a decent enough career, however, to be drafted by the Long Island Lizards in 2009, where he became a star. Adams was named MLL Goalie of the Year in 2011, 2012, and in 2015, when he led the Lizards to the league championship.

The Denver Outlaws' Jesse Schwartzman has two MLL Goaltender of the Year awards and the 2014 Steinfeld Cup win as MLL champions under his belt. Unlike Adams, Schwartzman had a remarkable career in college, starring for Johns Hopkins from 2004-2007. He won two national titles at JHU. In 2005, he backstopped the Blue Jays to an undefeated championship season. As a senior in 2007, they won another title. Schwartzman was NCAA tournament MVP both times.

Like Schwartzman, John Galloway had an impressive NCAA career. He played at the other lacrosse powerhouse, Syracuse, from 2008-2011, where he won NCAA Championships in 2008 and 2009. In his junior and senior seasons, he won the Kelly Award and was First Team All-American both years. As a pro, Galloway has been just as good. He was 2014 MLL

Jesse Schwartzman

Goaltender of the Year in leading Rochester to the final and was a 2015 MLL All-Star.

Tyler Fiorito also represented his MLL club in the 2015 All-Star game. Fiorito plays for the Chesapeake Bayhawks, with whom he served as the backup goalie for Steinfeld Cup wins in 2012 and 2013. He took over as full-time starter in 2015 and led the MLL in save percentage, finishing second in goals against average. Fiorito played NCAA lacrosse at Princeton, where he was a four-year starter from 2009-2012.

Jordan Burke played in just three games in his 2006 freshman year at Brown but had a stellar career as a starter from 2007-2009. In his senior year, he was a First Team All-American and the winner of the Kelly Award. Following the 2009 season, he was taken three spots ahead of Adams in the 2009 MLL draft by Boston. In 2011, he led the Cannons to a Steinfeld Cup and was chosen as MVP in the championship game.

Maryland vs. Loyola in the 2012 NCAA Men's
Division I Lacrosse Championship game

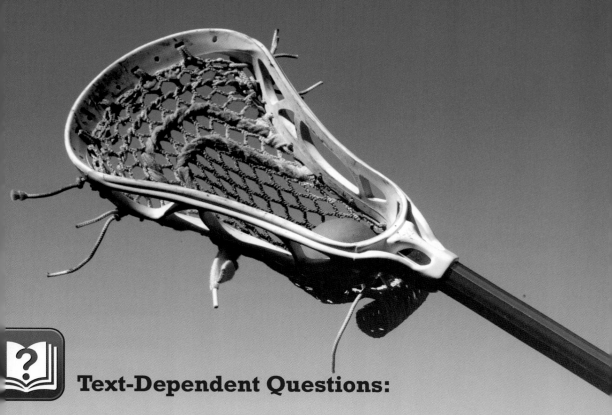

Text-Dependent Questions:

Which star player scored the record for NCAA single-season points?

Who was named First Team All-American in his junior and senior years when he also won the William C. Schmeisser Award, as the NCAA's best defenseman, then went on to be named an MLL All-Star in each of his first two pro seasons?

Which Denver Outlaws' goalie has two MLL Goaltender of the Year awards and the 2014 Steinfeld Cup win as an MLL champion under his belt?

Research Project:

Attend a high school lacrosse game. Take note of the players, and give your assessment on who has the greatest potential to play in college. How do the fans react to the best players, and in your opinion how does that affect the players?

DAVE PIETRAMALA

MICHAEL POWELL

CASEY POWELL

JOHN GRANT JR.

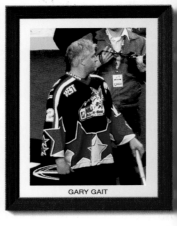

GARY GAIT

BRODIE MERRILL

The best players in the history of the U.S. game are inducted into the National Lacrosse Hall of Fame in Baltimore. Scan the code to the left to learn more about the men and women who are the legends of the sport.

CHAPTER 7

THE GREATEST PLAYERS IN LACROSSE HISTORY

Given the multitude of Native American athletes who played the game of lacrosse for centuries, it is impossible to know which person has been the greatest ever to play. What we have to work with are modern recollections and written accounts of games from when lacrosse became an organized sport in the 1930s.

Many great men have played the sport since then, but so have many great women. While men's lacrosse has dominated the sport's landscape, women have played since the turn of last century, and the NCAA has sanctioned the women's game since 1982. There are now more than 100 Division 1 women's programs.

Although a relatively new organized sport, NCAA women's lacrosse has produced some standout talent. Only two programs have won more than three women's championships: Maryland and Northwestern.

The Maryland program produced players like Jen Adams (1998-2001), the all-time NCAA leader in career points with 445. She scored a record 148 (including 88 goals) in the 2001 season alone, the year the Terrapins won the last of seven straight championships.

At Northwestern, Hannah Nielsen had a brilliant career from 2006-2009, setting the career NCAA assist record with 224, including 83 in 2009, when the Wildcats won their fifth straight championship. She also scored 59 goals that year for 142 points, second best all-time to Adams for a single season. Other great Northwestern women include Nielsen's teammates Shannon Smith and Kristen Kjellman, each with more than 300 career points.

Other great offensive players include Katie Rowan of Syracuse, Mary Key of Johns Hopkins, Gail Cummings of Temple and Marsha Florio of Penn State.

Of course, the game is not all about scoring, and players like defenders Rachel Becker of Princeton, Cherie Greer of Virginia, Tracy Stumpf of Maryland and goalie Alex Kehoe of Maryland were outstanding at keeping the ball away from opponents and out of their own goals.

While lacrosse is certainly a thriving and vibrant NCAA women's sport, this chapter will focus on the longer organized history of the men's game, dating back to the first players that made the game great.

ATTACKMEN

Back in the early 1930s, it was no small thing to be compared to baseball superstar Babe Ruth, whether the pursuit was athletic or otherwise. When Turnbull was called the "Babe Ruth of lacrosse," it meant no one had ever been better at attacking the lacrosse goal.

Turnbull was an attackman for Johns Hopkins University's lacrosse team from 1929-1932. A member of the National Lacrosse Hall of Fame, Turnbull's inductee profile describes his game this way: "He dodged and scored under tremendous defensive pressure; he fed with precision…and used a unique hip-check to put a defenseman with the ball on the ground." He was an All-American all three seasons at Johns Hopkins.

Mike French was also a three-time All-American in lacrosse. The Canadian-born French played forward for the Cornell University Big Red from 1974 to 1976. A prolific scorer in his NCAA career, he ranks third all-time in points per game and fourth in total career goals. He is one of only two players in NCAA history to average more than four goals per game.

In 1976, French had a season for the ages, scoring 65 goals and 105 points in leading Cornell to an undefeated season and an NCAA Championship. He won the Jack Turnbull Award as NCAA Attackman of the Year, and the Lt. Raymond Enners Award as the most outstanding player in men's NCAA lacrosse.

Casey Powell of West Carthage, NY, also won the Turnbull Award and the Enners Award in the same season as a member of the Syracuse Orangemen. Powell played at Syracuse from 1995-1998, where he was a three-time All-American.

In 1995, he helped Syracuse win the national championship. In 1996, he played midfielder, where he won the Lt. Donald McLaughlin Jr. Award as the most outstanding midfielder. He switched to forward in 1997, where he played when he won his first Enners Award. In his senior year of 1998, he won both the Turnbull and the Enners. Powell went on toa standout professional career, winning Major League Lacrosse's Offensive Player of the Year twice, in 2005 and again in 2014, a season in which he was also league MVP.

Powell's younger brother, Michael, followed his sibling's footsteps to Syracuse, and proceeded to outdo Casey's remarkable career. Mike was a four-time All-American at Syracuse from 2001-2004. He won the Turnbull Award in every one of his four seasons, a feat no one else has ever accomplished.

Mike Powell led his team to the NCAA Championship game three times, including his freshman year, where the Orangemen lost to Princeton. He helped his team triumph in the other appearances, however, winning titles in 2002 and 2004. In the 2004 season, he also won the Enners Award by scoring 89 points to become Syracuse's all-time leading scorer, and he is eighth all-time in NCAA scoring.

Like the Powells, the University of Delaware's John Grant Jr. also won the Enners Award. The difference is Grant did so in one of only two seasons in the NCAA. Grant, from Peterborough, Ontario, had played junior lacrosse in Ontario before going to junior college in the U.S. He transferred to Delaware in 1998, where he scored 40 goals and 67 points.

In 1999, he won the Enners Award by scoring 56 goals and 110 points, which is the seventh-best season total in NCAA history. He also ranks 13th in NCAA all-time points per game scored. Grant went on to have a stellar professional career, winning MLL Offensive Player of the Year three times, MVP twice, and five league titles.

Casey Powell

MIDDIES

The accolades for Gary Gait often include "best player in the history of the sport," and there are plenty of reasons to support the popularity of that opinion. Gait is from Victoria, British Columbia, on Canada's west coast. His NCAA career took him east to Syracuse, where Gait took college lacrosse by storm. His 192 career goals are the most ever for a midfielder and the third most in NCAA history.

Gait led the Orangemen to three straight NCAA titles from 1988-1990. Along the way, he won the McLaughlin Award in 1988 and 1989. In 1990, he added the Enners Award as MOP to his collection. In his professional career, he was MLL Rookie of the Year in 1991 and MLL MVP in 2005, the season in which his Baltimore Bayhawks won the MLL Championship.

Gary Gait

Gait cites playing for Syracuse coach Roy Simmons Jr. as the reason he chose to play for the Orangemen. Simmons spent his entire career at Syracuse, as a player, assistant coach,

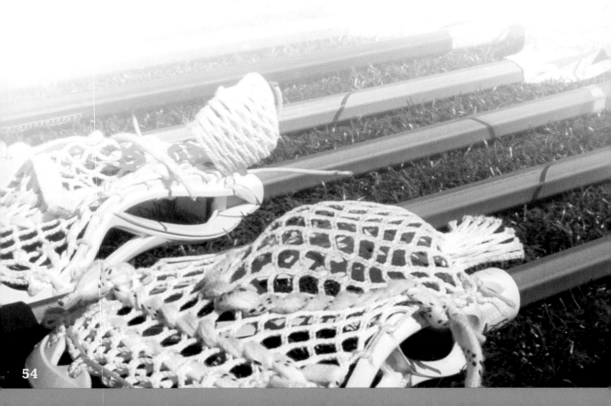

and head coach. When he played, he did so alongside a midfielder with even more athletic talent than Gait: future NFL Hall of Famer Jim Brown.

Brown was a standout high school lacrosse player in Manhasset, NY, before arriving at Syracuse in 1954. "With my bulk, and ability to match (opponents') speed, I could pretty much do what I wanted," the 225 lbs. Brown said. The Orangemen were undefeated in Brown's senior season in 1957, when he was a First Team All-American and second in scoring in the country.

Delverne "Del'" Dressel was a four-time All-American playing midfield at Johns Hopkins in the mid-1980s. Only five others have been named four-time All-Americans in NCAA men's lacrosse history. In both 1984 and 1985, Dressel won the McLaughlin Award as the NCAA's top midfielder. Also in both those seasons, the Blue Jays won the national championship, going undefeated in 1984.

Dressel left Hopkins as its career scoring leader at midfield. He was remarkably consistent, scoring at least 22 goals and 40 points every season. During his NCAA career, Dressel's teams lost a total of five games, all by a single goal. Dressel was inducted into the National Lacrosse Hall of Fame in 2002.

Huntington, NY, native Jay Jalbert had a Hall of Fame-worthy career as a midfielder at the University of Virginia in the late 1990s. Jalbert arrived in Charlottesville in 1997 as an All-American high school recruit. He hit his stride in 1998, scoring 34 goals as a sophomore. In 1999, he was named an All-American, as well as being named the McLaughlin Award winner. He capped the season by leading the Cavaliers to the NCAA Championship. In his senior season of 2000, Jalbert was named an All-American again.

Jalbert's professional career included four MLL All-Star selections and the 2003 MLL MVP award.

At the same time Jalbert was anchoring the Virginia midfield, Josh Sims was doing the same at Princeton. Arriving as a freshman from Annapolis, MD, Sims helped the Tigers to an undefeated season and their second consecutive national championship in 1997. As a sophomore in 1998, he received the first of three straight All-American selections and won the Mclaughlin Award. That year, Princeton won its third straight NCAA championship.

After his All-American senior season, in which Sims also won his second McLaughlin Award, Sims graduated to the professional game, where the stellar play and the winning continued. He is a five-time MLL All-Star and has won two league championships.

DEFENDERS

Hicksville, NY, native Dave Pietramala was a defensive stalwart for Johns Hopkins in the late 1980s. Pietramala is also known for accomplishing a feat in the sport that no one else has ever accomplished. In 1987, he won the NCAA Championship with the Blue Jays. In 2005, he was the head coach of the Blue Jays when they won another championship, making him the only man to ever win titles as both a player and head coach.

Pietramala won his player championship with the 1987 Blue Jays, his first of three consecutive All-American seasons. In 1988, he was also voted as the recipient of the William C. Schmeisser Award as the NCAA's Most Outstanding Defenseman. In 1989, he repeated as Schmeisser winner and won the Enners as MOP as well.

When Pietramala started his NCAA career, he had the perfect road map laid out for him showing just how impactful a defender could be. Tom Haus played his senior season at the University of North Carolina in 1987, the year he won his second consecutive and third overall Schmeisser Award. Haus, also a three-time All-American, is the only player in NCAA history to win three Schmeisser Awards.

Dave Pietramala

Brodie Merrill

Haus' best season was in 1986 when he was the backbone of a national championship team for the Tar Heels. To cap off the championship season, Haus also won the Enners Award that year as well.

Another Enners Award-winning defenseman, Princeton's David Morrow grew up a long way from the Ivy League in Troy, MI, near Detroit. His father ran a tubing shop, where Morrow spent hours learning how to tinker with and build things. In his junior season of 1992, Morrow and the team peaked, with the Tigers winning the national championship and Morrow winning the Schmeisser. Another Schmeisser and the Enner came in 1993.

In that 1992 season, Morrow made a contribution to the sport aside from his stellar defensive play. Tired of constantly breaking aluminum sticks, he spent some time in his father's shop working to develop a titanium model, which he debuted in Princeton's semifinal win over North Carolina. After graduation, Morrow went on to start his own business, developing and supplying titanium sticks, which are now the norm in the industry. In 2001, he also co-founded the MLL, providing a pro outlet for field lacrosse.

Thanks to Morrow, players like Orangeville, Ontario's, Brodie Merrill grew up playing with titanium sticks. He played his high school lacrosse in Connecticut, where he was an All-American and New England high school defensive player of the year during his senior season. He decided on Georgetown University for his NCAA career, where he was twice an All-American and won the Schmeisser as a senior in 2005.

Merrill continued his dominant play as a pro in Morrow's Major League Lacrosse, winning MLL Rookie of the Year in 2005. Merrill went on to win MLL Defensive Player of the Year in each of the next six seasons. He led his teams to three straight championship games from 2009-2011, winning the first two.

When Merrill was at Georgetown, Lee Zink was playing 17 miles away at the University of Maryland. The Darien, CT, native played there from 2001-2004. In his senior season, Zink was the best defensive player in the country, winning the Schmeisser Award.

Zink was a first-round draft pick in the MLL in 2004 and went on to have a standout career. Along with Merrill and Nick Polanco, he was named as a defender to the MLL 10th Anniversary Team. Zink was voted back-to-back MLL Defensive Player of the Year in 2012 and 2013, breaking Merrill's stranglehold on the award. Zink won a league title with Baltimore in 2005 and retired after winning another title with Denver in 2014.

GOALIES

Oren Lyons Jr. learned everything he knew about lacrosse from his father, Oren Lyons Sr. The family lived on the Onondaga Reservation, and Oren Sr. played goalkeeper for an Iroquois team. Oren Jr. watched and copied his father's moves, and honed his skills to the point where he was good enough to play for Syracuse in 1956.

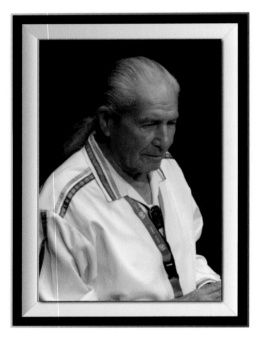

Oren Lyons Jr.

In 1957, Lyons was co-captain of the Orangemen team that claimed the ILA national championship. After graduation he continued to play club lacrosse for another dozen years. Lyons was inducted into the National Lacrosse Hall of Fame in 1992.

In 1992, Princeton goalie Scott Bacigalupo had a year that earned him the first of three consecutive Ensign C. Markland Kelly Jr. Awards as top men's NCAA goalkeeper of the season. The Brooklandville, MD, native played every game for the Tigers in his career from 1991-1994.

He not only won the Kelly Award from 1992-1994, but Bacigalupo also backstopped his team to national titles in 1992 and 1994. In each championship season, he was named the NCAA Men's Lacrosse Championship Tournament Most Outstanding Player. In 1994, he became only the third goalie ever to win the Enners Award. The championships were the first in lacrosse in Princeton history. Princeton had never qualified for the post season until Bacigalupo arrived.

When Bacigalupo's run as the best goalie in NCAA lacrosse ended with his graduation, Maryland junior Brian Dougherty seized the crown. The Philadelphia native led the Terrapins to the national title game in 1995, where they lost to Syracuse 13-9. Dougherty was still named tournament MVP. He also won the Kelly Award that season and repeated as Kelly Award winner in his senior year.

Upon graduation, he played in the MLL, winning his first MLL championship with Long Island in 2001. Dougherty won MLL Goaltender of the Year awards in 2003 with Long Island, and also in Philadelphia in 2006-2007 for his hometown Barrage. The 2006 and 2007 seasons also included two more MLL Championship wins. Dougherty was named as the goalie on the MLL 10th Anniversary Team.

he next goalie to inherit best-in-college honors was Brown University's Greg Cattrano. "The
at" won the Kelly Award in 1997, his senior year. The Long Island, NY, native was a two-time
l-American at Brown.

is pro lacrosse career began indoors with the National Lacrosse League, but Cattrano jumped
utside to the MLL for its inaugural season in 2001. He played for the Baltimore Bayhawks and
d them to each of the first three MLL Championship games. Cattrano won the Steinfeld Cup
ophy in consecutive years from 2002-2004, the last of these with the Philadelphia Barrage.
e also won three of the MLL's first four Goaltender of the Year awards, including 2002, when
e was named the only goalie in MLL history to win MVP.

'inning MVP awards tends to be tough to do for goalies in any sport, as these awards tend
 favor offensive players. That is part of what makes the career of Johns Hopkins goaltender
irry Quinn remarkable. Quinn played at Hopkins from 1982-1985 when the Blue Jays made
ur straight appearances in the NCAA Championship game.

 1982 and 1983, Hopkins lost in the final with Quinn on the bench. Quinn's fortunes changed
 1984 when he became starter and backstopped the Blue Jays to an undefeated season and
on not only the Kelly Award, but the Enners as well. In his senior year of 1985, Quinn and
opkins did lose one game but won another title. Quinn once again won both the Kelly and
nners Awards. He is the only goalie to win the Enners Award more than once.

Career Snapshots

Attack

JACK TURNBULL 1930-32

No stats available prior to 1950

#17 MIKE FRENCH 1974-76

191 goals
105 assists
296 points

#22 CASEY POWELL 1995-98

158 goals
129 assists
287 points

#24 JOHN GRANT JR. 1998-99

96 goals
81 assists
177 points

#0 MICHAEL POWELL 2001-2004

150 goals
157 assists
307 points

*Stats available for 1957 season only

Midfield

#56 JIM BROWN 1955-57*

55 goals
30 assists
85 points

#4 DELVERNE DRESSEL 1983-86

99 goals
75 assists
174 points

#22 GARRY GAIT 1987-90

192 goals
61 assists
253 points

#10 JAY JALBERT 1997-2000

112 goals
43 assists
155 points

#4 JOSH SIMS 1997-2000

103 goals
38 assists
141 points

Defense

#13 TOM HAUS 1983–87

6 goals
3 assists
245 ground balls

#43 DAVE PIETRAMALA 1986–89

3 goals
1 assist
170 ground balls

#29 LEE ZINK 2001–2004

1 goal
0 assists
138 ground balls

#17 BRODIE MERRILL 2002–2005

8 goals
5 assists
249 ground balls

Goaltender

#59 OREN LYONS JR. 1955–58*

10 wins
210 saves

#21 LARRY QUINN 1982–85

27 wins
462 saves
.673 save percentage

#10 SCOTT BACIGALUPO 1991–94

52 wins

#3 BRIAN DOUGHERTY 1993–96

31 wins
658 saves
.625 save percentage

#4 GREG CATTRANO 1994–97

25 wins
590 saves
.600 save percentage

Army's Brandon Butler (#3) goes up against Syracuse's Jovan Miller (#23) in this regular season game.

Words to Understand:

spurring: goading or urging someone or something to action, speed, or achievement

saturation: the act or result of supplying so much of something that no more is wanted

franchises: rights or licenses granted by a company to an individual or group to market its products or services in a specific territory

CHAPTER 8

THE FUTURE OF LACROSSE

At the college level, there can be no doubt that the future of lacrosse is bright, for both men and women. In 2012, the University of Michigan became the first traditional football school to add men's lacrosse since Notre Dame in 1981, **spurring** a boom in expansion that is poised to continue.

In 2016, Hampton University added a varsity men's lacrosse program. Five Division II schools and six Division III schools also added men's programs in 2016. On the women's side, it was four programs added for D1, four for D2 and six for D3. For 2017 and 2018, there are plans to add a men's program at D1 Cleveland State, plus programs at two D2 and six D3 schools. For the women, four new D1 programs are planned, along with three at D2 and three at D3.

Ohio State Buckeyes vs. Michigan Wolverines men's lacrosse game at Michigan Stadium in Ann Arbor, Michigan

WHY LACROSSE GROWS

What is prompting all these colleges to add the sport? One of the primary drivers is the growth at the high school level. The National Federation of State High School Associations data shows that between 2008 and 2013, high school lacrosse participation grew 19 percent among girls and 15 percent among boys. Among sports with at least 10,000 participants, that is the fastest growth rate in the country.

Colorado High School Lacrosse:
Denver East vs. George Washington

Lacrosse does have a reputation as a privileged, northeastern prep school sport. That may have been true 30 years ago, but between 2009 and 2013, Florida, Georgia, Virginia, Minnesota, Ohio and Michigan saw the most growth. This makes sense, because as the sport nears **saturation** in traditional areas, areas where it is new and underdeveloped will see faster growth rates.

SPREADING OUT

Strong growth in the South and Midwest may not necessarily be matched in all parts of the country, however. In Nebraska, for example, only eight high schools in the state have boy's teams. They can travel up to six hours to get to games. The state will not officially sanction the sport until 20 high schools in bordering states to the west and to the east play the sport. In the middle part of the country where population is sparser, and football is king, adding lacrosse might take decades. That only means, however, that there are untapped regions where growth can spread to once the current growth areas slow down.

Although not at the same scale as football, lacrosse is a contact sport, and there are concussion concerns. That aside, the sport is more appealing to the next generation of potential players and their parents. It is not as expensive to outfit as hockey and can be played on any soccer field, rather than requiring expensive ice time. It is a game of skill and athleticism, but there is no need to be tall, like in basketball, or big, like in football. Unlike baseball, it is fast and active, and there is way more scoring than in soccer, and kids love to score.

Lacrosse is also moving out of the suburbs, and colleges, especially ones with new programs, are actively trying to recruit athletes outside the traditional prep school mold. Programs like Harlem Lacrosse have brought the sport to schools in New York City and Baltimore, exposing a generation of kids to a sport they previously had never seen.

Lacrosse is a full contact sport, where body checking is permitted. Like football, it has come under scrutiny due to a heightened awareness of the effects of concussions.

Fifth Third Bank Stadium
Atlanta Blaze, Kennesaw, GA

Harvard Stadium
Boston Cannons, Boston, MA

American Legion Memorial Stadium
Charlotte Hounds, Charlotte, NC

Navy–Marine Corps Memorial Stadium
Chesapeake Bayhawks, Annapolis, MD

Sports Authority Field at Mile High
Denver Outlaws, Denver, CO

Florida Atlantic University Stadium
Florida Launch, Boca Raton, FL

Field lacrosse, the traditional form of the sport played outside in soccer or football stadiums, appears poised to endure and thrive into the future. The sport, however, has another form that brings a different perspective to the sport. Since 1987, professional lacrosse has existed in the form of indoor, or "box" lacrosse. The indoor version of the game differs in significant ways:

- the clock does not run when play is stopped

- teams on the field consist of six players per side

- like a hockey rink, the playing surface is surrounded by boards

- goals are two square feet smaller than field lacrosse goals, at 4' x 4'

- the playing surface is only 200' x 80'

- like hockey, the box game permits fighting

The National Lacrosse League is the most recent brand of box lacrosse and had 13 **franchises** in 2016. It has been around about 15 years longer than the MLL, but purists see it as a bastardization of the game rather than a progression. It is a rougher, tougher brand of lacrosse that has its own dedicated following.

INDOOR ASPIRATIONS

In the U.S. however, where the population with the ability to grow the sport exists, the box game is mostly viewed as an off-season training ground for the field version. The sport's governing body in the U.S., U.S. Lacrosse, does not support the indoor version of the game, citing a lack of time and resources due to the efforts put behind growing the field version.

For box lacrosse, the future may look much like it does now in Minneapolis. Minnesota is not a traditional lacrosse region, so when the pro indoor game came there (the Minnesota Swarm), the team set up a youth box league to spur

interest in the game. This participation led to increased interest in the high school field version, and to field players with refined skills learned playing the box version in winter. It is a model that could lead to the box version being viewed as a viable compliment to the field game in the U.S.

FUTURE STARS

RYAN CONRAD

The University of Virginia midfielder dreamed of playing for the Cavaliers despite growing up near lacrosse hotbed Baltimore. He had 55 points and 68 groundballs as an All-American at Loyola Blakefield prep school. At 6'0", 180 lbs., Conrad dominated with a left-to-right split dodge move that allowed him to gain separation from opponents. Quick and athletic, Conrad has worked with a specialized coach to improve his shot.

SERGIO PERKOVIC

The 2015 NCAA Tournament was a coming out party for the offensively minded Notre Dame sophomore midfielder. He led the Irish with 34 goals on the season. At 6'4", 220 lbs., the First Team All-American Sergio Perkovic is an imposing force, as he showed in the NCAA Tournament semifinal against Denver. Perkovic scored five goals in the fourth quarter of the game. Three of those came in a natural hat trick spanning just 1:35 on the clock to send the game to overtime.

Text-Dependent Questions:

In 2012, which university became the first traditional football school to add men's lacrosse since Notre Dame in 1981?

List the most significant ways that the indoor version of lacrosse differs from the traditional game played outside on a soccer or football field.

Give examples of two up-and-coming stars in lacrosse.

Research Project:

o online to obtain the statistics of high school participation in lacrosse. Create a chart howing key elements to the growth of the sport. What geographical regions are experiencing e greatest growth? What are the percentages of girls and boys playing the sport in those eas? What are the socioeconomic conditions in areas where lacrosse is most popular? ow many college scholarships are given to players in each of these areas?

GLOSSARY OF LACROSSE TERMS

adept: highly skilled.

attackman: an offensive player in lacrosse (one who tries to score).

backstopped: worked as a goalkeeper.

checked: being hit by another player as he or she tries to knock the ball away.

chronicle: to report, to describe the details of events.

continuity: something that doesn't change as it moves through time.

crease line: a line that curves around the goal, providing the goalie a place to block a shot or make a save and then clear the ball.

deflected: suddenly changing direction after having been hit.

definitive: complete, accurate, cannot be changed.

depictions: to show or describe with the use of a picture.

dominant: more successful or powerful than anyone else.

feat: an accomplishment requiring great skill, knowledge, or ability.

impactful: having a big effect.

innovations: a new idea, an invention.

instrumental: serving as a means to an end.

overshadowed: to make a situation less pleasurable or important when compared to or because of something else.

maneuvering: moving in a way to gain an advantage.

practitioner: a person who does something that requires specific skills or knowledge.

projections: educated guess about what will happen based on the present trends.

proximity: located close to.

refined: to improve, to make better.

sanction: to approve officially, to give permission.

standout: the best of something, for example, a most valuable player.

stellar: outstanding, having or done with great skill or ability.

transform: to change into something else, oftentimes for the better.

unprecedented: not having been done before.

vacate: to leave or to give up.

viability: capable of existing, even developing.

winger: a player positioned to the extreme right or left side of the field.

CHRONOLOGY

1636: A French missionary sees the Huron Indians playing lacrosse near Thunder Bay, Ontario, and becomes the first to document the game.

1834: Reports of a group of Indians demonstrating lacrosse for men from Montreal appear in the newspaper.

1860: Canadian dentist Dr. William Beers begins codifying rules for lacrosse.

1877: New York University fields the nation's first college lacrosse team.

1879: John R. Flannery earns the title "father of American lacrosse" by initiating the National Lacrosse Association.

1933: The number of players on a side is reduced from 12 to I 0.

1947: Position names in men's lacrosse are changed to goalkeeper, midfield, attack, and defense.

1948: Lacrosse is a demonstration sport at the Olympics in 1948 (London). Only England and the United States participate.

1971: Men's College lacrosse allies with the NCAA. The International Federation of Women's Lacrosse Association (IFWLA) is founded.

1971: The NCAA holds its first collegiate championship, with Cornell defeating the University of Maryland, 12-6.

1982: The first NCAA women's championship is played at Trenton State University between the University of Massachusetts and Trenton State University.

1987: Modern professional box lacrosse debuts with four teams.

1988: The National Lacrosse League merges with the MILL and begins play with eight teams.

1990: Coach Roy Simmons Jr. of Syracuse University is the first coach to win four NCAA titles.

1990: Jon Reese of Yale University sets the NCAA Men's Division I Lacrosse goals record with 82.

2001: The inaugural season of Major League Lacrosse is played.

001: Jen Adams of the University of Maryland breaks the all-time NCAA Women's Division Lacrosse career points record, scoring 445 over four seasons.

003: The NCAA Men's Championship is played in Baltimore's M&T Bank Stadium, marking the first time that the event is held in an NFL stadium.

003: The ILF and IFWLA U-19 World Championships are held in Towson, Maryland (U.S.) where the U.S. teams win both titles.

004: Lacrosse is named the official team sport of Maryland.

006: The International Lacrosse Federation World Championship is played in London, Ontario (Canada). The Canadians win the title with a 15-10 victory over the U.S. in the gold medal game, snapping the American men's 38-game winning streak, dating back to 1978.

008: The Federation of International Lacrosse (FIL) is formed through a merger of the men's and women's international lacrosse associations.

010: A record 29 nations participate in the FIL Men's World Championship in Manchester, England. The U.S. defeats Canada 12-10 in the gold medal game.

015: Lyle Thompson of the University of Albany breaks the all-time NCAA Men's Division I Lacrosse career points record, scoring 400 over four seasons.

015: The University of Denver wins the first-ever NCAA men's lacrosse championship by a school outside the Eastern Time Zone.

Lacrosse Today: In January 2016, Duke University senior midfielder Myles Jones was selected first overall in the Major League Lacrosse draft by the Atlanta Blaze. The McLaughlin Award winner is only the second black player ever to be drafted first overall, which is not surprising given that less than 10 percent of college players are black, according to the NCAA Student-Athlete Race/Ethnicity Report. In 2016, 29 organizations reaped the benefits of grants awarded by the U.S. Lacrosse Diversity & Inclusion Grant Program. The grants are awarded to initiate or continue lacrosse programs that promote diversity participation and education in underrepresented communities.

FURTHER READING

Fisher, Donald M. Lacrosse: *A History of the Game.* Baltimore, Maryland: Johns Hopkins University Press, 2011

Zimmerman, Don. *Men's Lacrosse.* Champaign, IL: Human Kinetics, 2013.

Wells, Don. *Lacrosse (In the Zone series).* New York, New York: Weigl Publishers, Incorporated, 2010.

INTERNET RESOURCES:

National Lacrosse Hall of Fame http://www.uslacrosse.org/about-us-lacrosse/hall-of-fame.aspx

NCAA Men's Division I Lacrosse http://www.ncaa.com/sports/lacrosse-men/d1

Major League Lacrosse http://www.majorleaguelacrosse.com/

Inside Lacrosse http://www.insidelacrosse.com/

VIDEO CREDITS:

Air Gait Goal (pg 8) https://www.youtube.com/watch?v=PmZ9lCPySyE

Hidden Ball Trick (pg 9) https://www.youtube.com/watch?v=VhXI421tz6A

1989 NCAA National Championship (pg 10) https://www.youtube.com/watch?v=FUntg7iXJs&list=PLQZJfoC8iUZ-vVD9RPWPW8SolcPSnNoFy&index=8

Moe is Money (pg 11) https://www.youtube.com/watch?v=OeR-6e_7KX0

The Tenth Title (pg 12) https://www.youtube.com/watch?v=Op7GNT17_Qc

Duke wins first NCAA championship (pg 13) https://www.youtube.com/watch?v=c8gLh8ZJijA

QR CODES AND LINKS TO THIRD-PARTY CONTENT

You may gain access to certain third-party content ("Third-Party Sites") by scanning and using the QR Codes that appear in this publication (the "QR Codes"). We do not operate or control in any respect any information, products, or services on such Third-Party Sites linked to by us via the QR Codes included in this publication and we assume no responsibility for any materials you may access using the QR Codes. Your use of the QR Codes may be subject to terms, limitations, or restrictions set forth in the applicable terms of use or otherwise established by the owners of the Third-Party Sites. Our linking to such Third-Party Sites via the QR Codes does not imply an endorsement or sponsorship of such Third-Party Sites, or the information, products or services offered on or through the Third-Party Sites, nor does it imply an endorsement or sponsorship of this publication by the owners of such Third-Party Sites.

PICTURE CREDITS

INDEX

In this index, page numbers in **bold italics** font indicate photos or videos.